MY DOG'S TALE

BY LORIE GLANTZ

ILLUSTRATIONS BY EMILY YOUNGREEN

DELACORTE

Illustrations on pages 20, 33, 91, and 103 by Pat Cheal
All other illustrations by Emily Youngreen

Poem reprinted from THE SOULS OF ANIMALS
by Gary Kowalski with permission from
Stillpoint Publishing

Published by
Delacorte Press
Random House, Inc.
1540 Broadway
New York, New York 10036

Delacorte Press® is a registered trademark
of Random House, Inc., and the colophon is a trademark
of Random House, Inc.

ISBN 0-385-33536-9

Manufactured in the United States of America.
Published simultaneously in Canada.

October 2000

10 9 8 7 6 5 4 3 2 1
RRH

DEDICATIONS

*To Reef, my first special guy, the memories of the times
we shared will live with me forever. You instilled in me the importance of always looking at things from the other perspective.*

*To Zipper, my incredible golden one, you are truly a part of
my soul. Our journey together has taught me to recognize and
cherish the everyday, spectacular moments in life.*

ACKNOWLEDGMENTS

FIRST, I WOULD LIKE TO THANK Bea Moore who helped inspire this book. Her love, dedication, and giving never cease to amaze me. To my parents, you have been fundamental in the journey of my life.

To Nolan, thank you for your love, faith, and hard work. To Brian and Laura, thank you for letting me bend your ears. To Max and Marcia, your counsel was invaluable. To my grandmother Katherine, you have always made me feel special and loved; thank you for all that you have done for me. Last but not least, to my son Zachary, I am so glad our journey together has just begun.

To Glen Edelstein, thank you for helping this book stay on course. A sincere thanks to Larry Wengren and all my alpha readers for reviewing my manuscripts. A special thanks to Emily Youngreen and Pat Cheal whose wonderful illustrations grace the pages of this book. Emily, thank you for breathing life into my thoughts. To Joel Avirom, your talent is clearly seen in the design of this book. To my agent, Meredith Bernstein, thank you for seeing my vision and teaching me by example. To my editor, Danielle Perez, who helped me along the bumpy road of publication and has answered my endless list of questions—I thank you for your understanding.

THIS BOOK IS A JOURNAL OF
THE LIFE AND TIMES OF MY DOG

. . . .

I BEGAN CREATING THIS JOURNAL ON

. . . .

IF FOR ANY REASON THIS JOURNAL GETS LOST,
PLEASE CONTACT ME AT:

. . . .

. . . .

. . . .

Puppy's Birthday

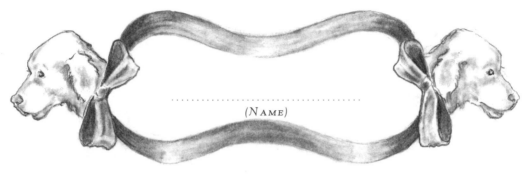

....
(Name)

Was born on

....

In the year

....

At birth our puppy weighed

....

(lbs./ozs.)

Our puppy is a

....

(boy/girl)

and is a

....

(breed)

Everyone needs a spiritual guide: a minister,
rabbi, counselor, wise friend, or therapist.
My own wise friend is my dog.
He has deep knowledge to impart.
He makes friends easily and doesn't hold a grudge.
He enjoys simple pleasures and takes each day as it comes. . . .
Best of all, he befriends me with an unconditional love
that human beings would do well to imitate.

—GARY KOWALSKI

My Dog's Tale is a journal of many things. Most importantly, it is a journal of your incredible relationship with your dog. In tracking the everyday events and the milestones that shape your dog's life, you create a permanent document that honors and cherishes the bond you have with your dog. It is my greatest hope that creating this journal will give you joy and enrich your relationship with your dog.

FAVORITE DOGGIE PICTURES

ADOPTING A NEW FAMILY MEMBER

CONGRATULATIONS! BY THE TIME you are reading this, you probably have decided to adopt a dog or are living with one already. By doing so, you have made a decision to extend your family, which now includes a wonderful canine that will add tremendous joy to your life. With this enjoyment comes responsibility and hard work. For most of us, all the hard work pales in comparison with the love and spiritual nourishment that we get from our relationships with our dogs.

The bonds we have with our dogs are rewardingly comfortable and pure. There are few relationships in life that can match the ones we have with our dogs. Our dogs possess the ability to lift our spirits, to share our deepest secrets, and to make us laugh.

Life just seems better when you share it with a dog. Dogs seem to have a way of bringing out the best in us—somehow we are more human when we are with them. Whether you have experienced these feelings yet or not, one thing is for sure—you are about to embark upon a journey that will change and shape your life in powerful ways, ways that you cannot even imagine.

Pooch Pointer: Scenting of an Object

If you get your dog from a breeder, before you bring your dog home, take a soft toy or towel to the breeder's. Have the breeder leave the item with the litter to get the scent of the mother and siblings on it. If you get your dog from a shelter or another source, try to bring home something from the dog's previous residence. A familiar scent will make the transition much easier for the dog. Place this object in the dog's area in your home.

Choosing a Name

CHOOSING A NAME FOR THE NEW MEMBER of your family is a very personal and important decision. This process can be both fun and frustrating at the same time. The bottom line is, pick a name that you like.

Tips for Choosing a Name

- It is best to keep the call name, the name you will use every day for the dog, to one or two syllables.

- Try to pick a name that doesn't sound similar to either a word that is used often in normal conversation or a command you would give your dog.

- Think of themes that are important in your life (e.g., the outdoors, sports, or music); then generate a list of words that you associate with those themes.

- If you decide on the name of your pup before you actually get him, give the name that you choose time to settle in. Even say it out loud to see how it sounds.

- If you don't decide on a name before you get your pup, you may be able to generate some ideas for a name based on the dog's personality or markings.

Pooch Pointer:
Teaching Your Puppy His Name

When talking to your puppy, say his name often. If he looks at you after you say his name, smile at him and praise him.

The Puppy's Name

We named our puppy

. . . .

On

. . . .

How we chose our puppy's name

. . . .

. . . .

. . . .

The special significance of our puppy's name

. . . .

. . . .

. . . .

Other names that we considered

. . . .

. . . .

. . . .

. . . .

LITTER MATES

Puppy's name . . . .
Gender . . . .
Owner's name . . . .
Address . . . .
. . . .
Phone . . . .
E-mail address . . . .

Puppy's name . . . .
Gender . . . .
Owner's name . . . .
Address . . . .
. . . .
Phone . . . .
E-mail address . . . .

Puppy's name . . . .
Gender . . . .
Owner's name . . . .
Address . . . .
. . . .
Phone . . . .
E-mail address . . . .

Puppy's name . . . .
Gender . . . .
Owner's name . . . .
Address . . . .
. . . .
Phone . . . .
E-mail address . . . .

Puppy's name . . . .
Gender . . . .
Owner's name . . . .
Address . . . .
. . . .
Phone . . . .
E-mail address . . . .

Puppy's name . . . .
Gender . . . .
Owner's name . . . .
Address . . . .
. . . .
Phone . . . .
E-mail address . . . .

CANINE FAMILY TREE

OUR DOG

....
Name

....
Date of Birth

....
Breed

MOTHER

....
Name

....
Date of Birth

....
Breed

....
Owner

....
Address

....
Phone

....
E-Mail

FATHER

....
Name

....
Date of Birth

....
Breed

....
Owner

....
Address

....
Phone

....
E-Mail

Preparations Before Bringing Home a Puppy

Puppy-Proofing

HAVING A PUPPY IS A GREAT WAY to keep your house picked up because anything left within reach is fair game. Puppies can get into all kinds of trouble in the blink of an eye.

One of the best ways to puppy-proof is to get down on your hands and knees and crawl around your house and yard (if you're up to it). This gives you a very good idea of what your puppy is going to be seeing.

Anything that you think your puppy might chew, he probably will. Close all doors leading to rooms to which you don't want your puppy to have access; don't forget to close closet doors. Move all dangerous or valuable chewable items out of reach, and out of the range of temptation!

PUPPY-PROOFING CHECKLIST

The House

- Secure cleaning products, chemicals, and medications, especially in your kitchen and bathroom.

- Tack down electrical cords (TV, VCR, lamps, stereo, computer/printer, etc.), or cover them with something to deter chewing. Use aluminum foil or Bitter Apple®, a product you apply (spray or foam) to make objects taste bitter.

- Secure knickknacks. Clear low shelves and tables, such as coffee tables and end tables, of dangerous and breakable objects.

- Make sure the trash can and recycling bins are inaccessible.

> ## Pooch Pointer: Garbage Cans
>
> *Do not dispose of medicine or dangerous items in trash cans that do not have secure lids (e.g., bathroom wastepaper baskets).*

The Garage

- Store any stray boxes or loose materials, such as tools, nails, and screws.

- Secure any chemicals or toxic compounds, including but not limited to: paint, thinner, gasoline, antifreeze.

> ## Pooch Pointer: A Microchip for Your Dog
>
> *Having a microchip implanted in your dog is an effective tool to reunite you if he is ever lost, especially if your dog is an escape artist. The implantation is relatively inexpensive and painless.*

The Yard

Take a careful look at your yard. Is it safe for a dog? If you have a fence, is it secure?

Things to check and secure in your yard:

- Garden tools/hoses
- Holes in ground
- Lawn furniture
- Standing water
- Fertilizer
- Storage shed
- Pool/hot tub
- Excess lumber or metal

Check any fences for:

- Holes
- Loose boards
- Insecure gates

Do you have any dangerous plants? Many common plants can be toxic and sometimes fatal to dogs. If you are not sure whether a plant or compound is toxic to your dog, call your vet. You can also call the ASPCA National Animal Poison Control Center. Consultations can be charged to your credit card by calling 1-800-548-2423 or to your phone bill at 1-900-680-0000. The list below is a partial list of plants with toxic substances (*Guide to Poisonous and Toxic Plants*, U.S. Army Center for Health Promotion and Preventive Medicine, 1998).

TOXIC PLANTS, TREES, AND SHRUBS

Azalea
Buttercup
Caladium and
    elephant's ear
Delphinium
Dieffenbachia
    (dumb cane)
English ivy
Holly berry and
    holly bush
Hydrangea
Jasmine (berries)
Larkspur
Lily of the valley
Morning glory
Oleander
Philodendron
Rhododendron
Wisteria
Yew

TOXIC BULBS

Daffodil
Hyacinth
Iris
Lily
Narcissus

TOXIC SEEDS AND PITS

Apple seeds
Apricot pits
Peach pits
Plum pits

TOXIC WILD PLANTS

Elderberry
Mushrooms
Toadstools

ESSENTIAL SUPPLIES

YOU SHOULD ACQUIRE THESE SUPPLIES before bringing your new puppy home.

Puppy Food

- High-quality puppy food is best. Ask your vet for a recommendation. At first, buy a small quantity of food to make sure your pup likes it.

Tip-Proof Food and Water Bowls

- Ceramic or stainless steel is best. Some stainless steel bowls even come with rubber edges that prevent the bowl from sliding.

- Size of bowls: keep in mind how large your dog will be at maturity.

- Beware of cheaper bowls, which your dog could chew.

Collars, Leashes, and Identification

- Begin with a lightweight nylon buckle collar. The length of the collar depends on the size of the pup's neck. Small breeds may need a harness.

- A six-foot leather leash is best. Width of leash depends on breed of dog.

- Ask your vet where to order an identification tag.

Pooch Pointer: Adjusting the Collar

To determine how the collar should fit, follow this rule of thumb: you should be able to place two fingers (side by side) between your dog's neck and the collar when the collar is resting at the bottom of the dog's neck. Make sure that you cannot slip the collar off over the dog's head.

Crate I cannot stress enough the importance of crate training your pup. This training will make your life with your pup much more enjoyable. Crate training means that you condition your dog to spend time in a crate. In case you are unfamiliar with crates, a crate is an enclosed box structure with ventilated sides and a secure door. Crates are made of either heavy-duty plastic with heavy wire windows for ventilation or heavy wire throughout. For the benefits of crate training, see page 88.

Dog Bed Make sure it is totally machine washable or has a removable cover that you can throw in the wash.

Toys

Bones Sterilized bones or Nylabones® are best.

Kongs® These are highly recommended. Put a biscuit or some peanut butter in the center—this will occupy your dog for a long time. But remember to remove it if your dog doesn't eat it.

Pooch Pointer: Toy Safety

When giving your pup a toy it is best to supervise the pup to see if the toy can stand up to your puppy. Never leave the puppy alone with a toy that can be chewed into shreds and ingested.

Soft Toys These are great comfort toys; almost every dog has a beloved one. If your dog tends to mouth a lot, keep a few of these toys around so that he has something to hold in his mouth when he gets excited (such as when someone comes to the door).

Balls Size is the issue here—don't let your puppy play with a ball that is small enough to be swallowed. Tennis balls are your best bet.

HIGHLY SUGGESTED SUPPLIES

GROOMING TOOLS AND TIPS

Brush, Comb, Undercoat Rake (for longhaired breeds), Flea Comb and Scissors Brush your dog daily, if possible, to remove dead hair and to keep your dog's skin healthy.

Nail Trimmer and Kwik Stop® (for nail trimming) Clip your dog's nails at least once a month. Ask your vet to show you how. Be sure to avoid clipping the "quick" (the blood vessel in the nail), which will bleed if cut. If you do cut the quick, put some Kwik Stop® on the nail to stop the bleeding.

Pet Toothbrush and Toothpaste Brush your dog's teeth at least once a week. Buy a kit, which contains a dog toothbrush and paste. Or use a regular small soft-bristled toothbrush with dog toothpaste. Do not use regular toothpaste on your dog.

Ear Cleaner Check your puppy's ears once a week. If you see any discharge, speak to your vet.

Shampoo and Conditioner Ask your vet how often to bathe your puppy.

Chemical Deodorizers/Neutralizers All dogs have "accidents." It's important to eliminate the scent of urine so that the dog doesn't continue to eliminate in the same spot. You can either buy commercial "odor neutralizer" products or make your own.

Baby Gates These are great for keeping your puppy confined to a certain area of the house.

Pooch Pointer: Making Your Own Deodorizer

Make a solution of half water and half white vinegar, and put it into a spray bottle. Use paper towels to pick up or soak up the "accident." Then spray solution onto the soiled area, rub, and then pat dry.

Questions to Ask Before the Puppy Moves In

ASK THE BREEDER, SHELTER, or rescue agency these questions before you take your new puppy home with you.

Food

- Ask for a small amount of the pup's food to bring home; this will make the transition smoother.

Personality

- Ask about your dog's personality traits. Is the pup dominant or submissive around people or other pups?

Health

- Ask for a current written record of immunizations and dewormings.
- Ask for a recommendation for a veterinarian in your area, if the pup's current vet is too far away.

Additional Questions for a Breeder

- If your pup is a purebred, ask for copies of the parents' health clearances and pedigrees. Also ask for an American Kennel Club (AKC) registration form to register or transfer ownership of your dog.

Questions for a Shelter or a Rescue Organization

- Ask if there are any issues (e.g., abuse, neglect) of which you should be aware.

> ### Pooch Pointer: Finding a Breeder
>
> *If you will be getting your puppy from a breeder, be sure that the breeder is reputable. One way to tell is that a reputable breeder will probably ask you to sign a sales contract that outlines your responsibilities as an owner. Your puppy should be at least seven weeks old before coming home.*

THINGS TO DECIDE BEFORE THE PUPPY COMES HOME

Do I have time to devote to a puppy?

Puppies need a lot of love, care, and attention. You will spend a lot of time in the beginning teaching the puppy "the ropes," especially when she first comes home. By doing this, you will reap the rewards of many enjoyable years of canine love.

Where is the pup going to sleep?

Keeping your puppy's bed or crate in your bedroom will allow you to form a stronger bond with your dog.

Where am I going to keep the pup when I am not at home?

Keeping the puppy in a crate is best and is safest for your puppy. However, blocking off your kitchen or a bathroom with baby gates is an OK choice. You must leave your puppy some paper to eliminate on. See page 32 for more information.

Think safety. Make sure that everything that could be chewed or eaten is removed or covered with a repellent like Bitter Apple®. Always remove the puppy's collar when he is home alone to prevent it from getting caught on something.

Pooch Pointer: First Car Ride Home

It is best to transport your new puppy home in a crate. After you get home, carry the pup directly to the soiling area. Once the pup is finished, praise her enthusiastically.

Puppy's First Day Home

Today

. . . .

WE ADOPTED OUR NEW PUPPY

. . . .

During the car ride home, our puppy . . . .

. . . .

. . . .

. . . .

. . . .

. . . .

. . . .

I will never forget . . . .

. . . .

. . . .

. . . .

. . . .

. . . .

. . . .

. . . .

Some of the things we did that day were . . . .

. . . .

. . . .

. . . .

. . . .

. . . .

. . . .

. . . .

. . . .

. . . .

. . . .

Pooch Pointer: First Day

Keep your puppy's first few days at home quiet; wait a few days to have guests over. Let the pup explore her new surroundings while you follow behind. Do not let the puppy roam around the house alone: you need to keep her out of trouble. Expect the pup to take several naps; have a safe area for this. Either block off part of the kitchen, or place her crate in the kitchen. Having the pup sleep in the kitchen allows the pup to get used to the sounds of daily activity. Also, don't forget to call the vet to schedule a checkup.

Puppy's First Night Home

We fell asleep . . . .

. . . .

. . . .

. . . .

. . . .

. . . .

During the night the puppy . . . .

. . . .

. . . .

. . . .

. . . .

. . . .

. . . .

The next morning . . . .

. . . .

. . . .

. . . .

. . . .

. . . .

. . . .

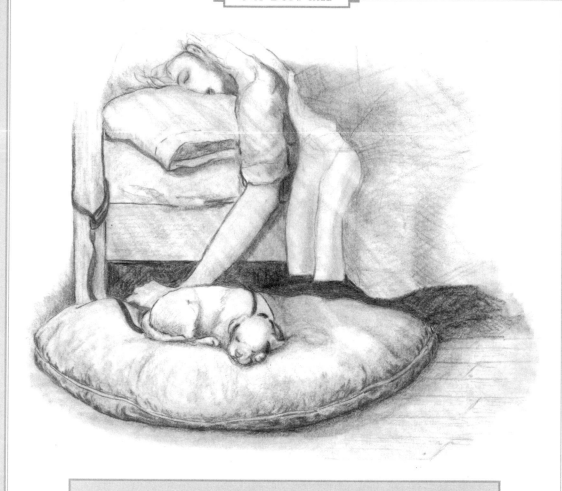

Pooch Pointer: First Night

Place the puppy's bed or a blanket next to your bed. Put on the pup's collar and leash, and tie him to your bed. Give the pup just enough slack to move around comfortably. Being close to you will allow your pup to calm down and bond with you. If you had the chance to bring a towel or toy to the breeder's to get the scent of the litter on it, be sure to have it next to the puppy. Sleep in a pair of sweats, and leave your shoes by the bed (but not near the pup)—you will be getting up to take the puppy outside to go potty. After the first few nights, your pup can sleep in a crate next to your bed.

THE EARLY DAYS

Paw Prints

Making the Paw Prints

Be aware that this could get a bit messy, so do this project outside or in an area of your house that is "dog safe." If you're doing it indoors, lay down newspapers before you begin. Have a bowl of warm soapy water and a few old towels close by. Take a standard ink pad and place your dog's paw firmly on the pad a few times. Then carefully place your dog's paw in the center of the appropriate square, and gently push down. After you're done with each paw, dip the paw in the soapy water and wipe it off. This can be quite a challenging project—so good luck!

Left Front Paw

Right Front Paw

Left Rear Paw

Right Rear Paw

Date:

HOUSEBREAKING A PUPPY

HOUSEBREAKING TIPS

YOUR PUPPY LEARNS BEHAVIORS by repetition, so begin to build a potty ritual the first day home. Also, consider crate training your pup. See page 88.

- Put your pup on a leash and go outside with your pup. Take the pup outside in the same way each time (e.g., out the same door).

- Once your pup has some control, begin to teach the pup a "potty signal," like sitting at the door before going outside. Eventually the pup will associate sitting at the door with being let outside.

- Just as the pup begins to eliminate, say your "potty command" (see Pooch Pointer below). After the pup finishes, praise him enthusiastically and reward him with a treat.

- If after five minutes your puppy will not go, take him inside. Watch him carefully or put him in the crate. Let ten minutes go by; then take him back outside.

- Do not expect the pup to be accident-free right away. Be patient. Never get angry with your pup, and never "rub your puppy's nose in it."

- Expect to take the puppy out during the middle of the night for the first few weeks.

Pooch Pointer: Choosing a Potty Command

Choose a command to encourage your pup to eliminate, such as "Go potty," "Hurry up," or "Get busy." Your pup will learn to associate the command with going potty. Then you can use the command to let the pup know what you would like him to do. This is very useful at two o'clock in the morning or in climates that get very cold in the winter.

Tips for avoiding an accident:

- Always keep the pup in the same room with you when the pup isn't in a potty-safe area.

- When you see the pup start to squat, say "No" and take the pup to the soiling area immediately.

- Set a potty schedule. Also, anticipate times that the puppy might have to go, such as:

  > First thing in the morning and just before you go to bed.

  > Whenever the pup wakes up from a nap or comes out of the crate.

  > After every meal and play session.

- Watch your pup's body language—you will learn the warning signs.

- Feed the pup a few hours before bedtime, and don't let him drink a lot right before bed.

When you're away at work:

- Arrange for someone to let your puppy out, or go home several times a day, because a puppy cannot hold it more than two to three hours during the day.

- Make sure the puppy-safe area (hopefully a crate) has a small amount of water in a tip-proof bowl and safe chew toys.

- If you are not crate training, place a layer of newspaper on the ground, away from the puppy's bed. Cover this with a layer that is shredded by hand into strips.

STARTING OFF ON THE RIGHT PAW

HERE ARE SOME TIPS TO HELP your puppy begin learning good habits right from the start.

Socializing

- Slowly and safely introduce the pup to many new experiences. If your puppy isn't fully vaccinated, ask your vet how to protect your pup.

- Keep your puppy accustomed to people of all ages.

- Invite friends over who have dogs that you can trust being around your pup. While your puppy is with another dog, carefully watch what is going on. Stop any aggressive behavior as soon as it starts.

- Puppies go through a fear period around ten weeks of age. During this phase, approach new situations with caution.

Mealtime

- It is very important to establish the fact that humans are not a threat to the pup's food, especially if you have children. Start by petting the puppy while he eats. Every once in a while, stick your hands in the food. Always praise the puppy if he submits to your actions. If at any point the dog growls or tries to nip, say "No" in a stern voice. Then resume the behavior that you were doing when the pup growled at you. A word of caution: If the puppy is very resistant to your corrections or if you have adopted an older dog, do not attempt this training yourself—seek the advice of a professional dog trainer.

Noise Conditioning

■ If your pup is startled by a noise, in a normal voice tell the pup "It's OK," and go on with what you were doing. Do not overreact to the situation.

Touch Conditioning

■ Pet, touch, hug, cuddle, and love your puppy on a daily basis.

■ Touch his paws, especially in between his toes. Look in his ears, and open his lips to look at his teeth. This makes trips to the vet and groomer easier.

Pooch Pointer: Puppy Class

The goal of puppy class is continued socialization, not formal training. Most classes require that your puppy is at least three months old. When choosing a class, make sure that all pups must be vaccinated in order to attend. These classes are not only valuable, they are also fun!

Puppy "Faux Paws"

Consistency and positive reinforcement are the keys to training. Always give an appropriate correction in response to any undesirable behavior, immediately when it happens, not after the fact. Likewise, you should always reward positive behavior, either with praise or a treat, immediately after it happens. This helps your dog identify desired and undesired behaviors. Once your dog has learned a particular behavior, you can reward him intermittently with a treat, but always try to reward him with praise.

Mouthing or Nipping

Puppies have razor-sharp teeth; when they mouth or nip, it can hurt, even draw blood. Pups need to learn that it isn't OK to mouth or nip at people.

Techniques to correct mouthing:

- When the pup mouths you, say "No bite" or "Ouch" in a firm and serious voice. As soon as he stops mouthing, praise him.

- If your pup isn't responding to the technique above, try this process. As soon as the pup mouths, again say "No bite" or "Ouch" in a firm and serious voice. Immediately stand up and ignore your puppy—now he has no one to play with. After a few minutes you can resume playing with him.

JUMPING UP

Jumping up can be initially thought of as a sign of affection. However, this behavior gets tiresome and can be dangerous.

A technique to correct jumping up:

■ Try to teach your dog to sit, instead of jumping up, when greeting people. If you're having trouble, put your puppy on his leash. Hold on to the leash, leaving your pup some slack but little enough that he won't be able to jump up. As your pup lifts his paws off the ground, the leash will become taut and pull him back down; at that moment say "Off." As soon as he has all four paws on the ground, praise him.

Pooch Pointer: Greeting a Jumping Puppy

Most puppies jump up to get attention. So, when you greet your puppy, bend down to his level and ask him to sit.

CHEWING

Most dogs chew; it is one way they investigate the world around them. Inappropriate chewing can be a very destructive and dangerous habit.

A technique to teach positive chewing behavior:

- Begin by quietly following your pup around the house.

- When the pup starts chewing on something that is inappropriate, say "No"; then take the object away and give the pup an acceptable replacement object to chew.

- When the pup chews this item, praise the puppy!

Techniques to prevent chewing problems:

- Most dogs chew because of boredom or anxiety, so making sure that your dog gets enough exercise and playtime can dramatically reduce a number of behavior problems. Until the dog is 14 months old, the best forms of exercise are swimming, short walks, free play, or fetch.

- Make sure that the dog has enough toys around the house to keep him mentally stimulated.

- If your dog seems to be getting bored with his toys, pick up some toys and put them in a drawer for a week. Then reintroduce them to your dog.

- When you leave an untrained dog home alone, make sure that he is in a safe area with lots of chew toys!

Pooch Pointer: Choice of Chew Toys

It is not a good idea to give your dog old shoes or socks to play with because it will teach him that it is OK to chew on similar things. You cannot expect your dog to be able to tell the difference between old and new shoes.

Seeing Is Believing

A Photographic Growth Chart

EVERY TWO MONTHS for the puppy's first year, take a photograph of your pup with the same toy. Take the picture in the same place each time. Make sure that you always stand about four feet away from your pup when you take each of the pictures. When you take the photograph, either kneel down or sit down on the ground; you want to be eye level with your puppy. After one year, you will have a visual growth chart for your dog, and you will also be able to see how your dog's toy stands the test of time. Note. Plan to crop the photos to fit them all on the next two pages.

HEIGHT GROWTH CHART

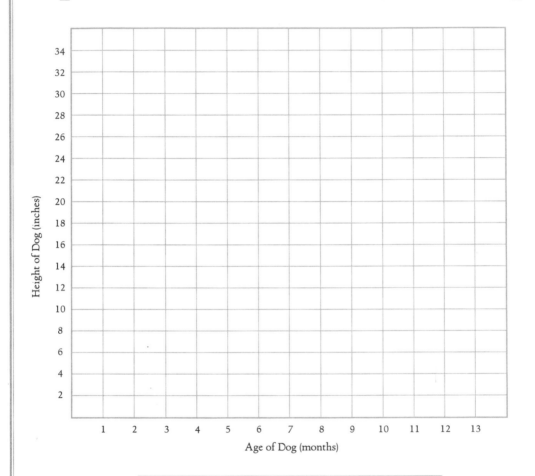

Height of Dog (inches)

34
32
30
28
26
24
22
20
18
16
14
12
10
8
6
4
2

1 2 3 4 5 6 7 8 9 10 11 12 13

Age of Dog (months)

Pooch Pointer: Doggie Sizes

Dogs come in all different shapes and sizes.
The Miniature Dachshund and the Maltese
are among the smallest breeds, standing only
5–9 inches tall. The Irish Wolfhound and the
Great Dane are among the largest breeds,
standing 30–34 inches tall.

Weight Gain Chart

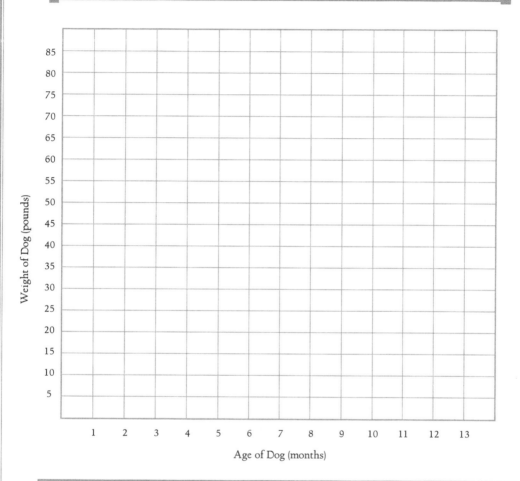

Weight of Dog (pounds)

85
80
75
70
65
60
55
50
45
40
35
30
25
20
15
10
5

1 2 3 4 5 6 7 8 9 10 11 12 13

Age of Dog (months)

Pooch Pointer: How to Tell If Your Dog Is Too Fat

While standing, put your dog between your legs. Bend over, reach your hands down, and place them on both sides of your dog's rib cage. Rub your hands back and forth over your dog's ribs. You should be able to feel the ribs easily, without applying too much pressure. This is just a guideline—before restricting your dog's diet, consult your veterinarian, as there may be other factors to consider in maintaining your dog's optimal health.

MEMORABLE FIRSTS

First car trip   Date . . . .

. . . .

. . . .

. . . .

. . . .

First trip to vet   Date . . . .

. . . .

. . . .

. . . .

. . . .

First walk   Date . . . .

. . . .

. . . .

. . . .

. . . .

First learned to swim   Date . . . .

. . . .

. . . .

. . . .

. . . .

First learned to fetch   Date . . . .

. . . .

. . . .

. . . .

. . . .

First time . . . .   Date . . . .

. . . .

. . . .

. . . .

. . . .

First time . . . .   Date . . . .

. . . .

. . . .

. . . .

. . . .

Pooch Pointer: Swimming

Never force your dog into a body of water. If your dog enjoys swimming, encourage your dog to swim—it's great exercise. If your dog swims in a pool, make sure you rinse your dog off when she comes out to protect her skin and coat from chlorinated water.

The First Bath

Date . . . .

My puppy's first bath . . . .

. . . .

. . . .

. . . .

. . . .

Pooch Pointer: Bathing Your Puppy

It is important that your puppy doesn't get chilled after coming out of the bath. Make sure your pup is dried off well. After toweling the puppy off, you might want to wrap the pup in a towel that you have warmed in the dryer. You can also blow-dry your puppy on the lowest heat setting of your hair dryer to keep the pup from getting a chill; always keep the dryer moving to avoid burns.

WALKING THE DOG

TAKING YOUR PUPPY FOR THE FIRST WALK is a much anticipated event. Although you should enjoy this time, you need to prepare for this walk. If your puppy isn't fully vaccinated, it is important to talk to your vet before taking your pup for a walk.

INTRODUCING YOUR PUP TO A COLLAR AND A LEASH

- You can slowly begin to introduce your pup to his collar as soon as he comes home. Do not have any identification tags on the collar at this time.

- If the pup scratches at the collar, distract him by playing with him.

- Once your pup is used to the collar, attach the leash and let the puppy drag it around the house for five minutes at a time. Follow behind to make sure the leash doesn't get caught on anything and to make sure the pup doesn't chew on the leash. If the pup chews on the leash, say "No" in a firm voice. Do this exercise twice a day for a few days.

- While the pup is dragging the leash around the house, pick up the leash and hold it loosely. Let the pup continue to wander around the house. Do this for about five minutes. Now change roles; have the pup follow you around the house for five minutes—either hold the leash or attach it to your belt loop. This teaches the pup that you are the leader.

- Gradually increase the amount of time the pup is wearing the leash. After the pup is comfortable following you around, introduce the "Let's go" command. "Let's go" is a signal to your dog to pay attention because we are about to move. Combine this command with a few pats of your hand against your hip, and begin to walk. Try to walk with your dog on your left.

■ If your pup is ignoring you or pulling at the leash, don't pull back on the leash. Try raising the pitch of your voice, and say "Let's go" followed by your dog's name. This should get the pup's attention. If this doesn't work, quickly walk in the opposite direction. If the pup is still pulling or seems frustrated, bend down, clap your hands, and call your puppy to you. When the pup starts walking to you, open your arms and praise him. Ask him to sit and then try walking again.

> ## Pooch Pointer: Identification Tags
>
> *Never leave the house without your pup's identification tags on her collar.*

The Mechanics of the First "Real" Walk

■ Make the first walk short in duration.

■ Always carry a few plastic bags in your pocket to pick up after your dog.

■ Have treats in your pocket, as this will allow you to reinforce the desired behaviors.

■ If the pup is straining at the end of the leash, quickly turn around and walk in the other direction. At the same time, call your pup's name and say "Let's go" while you pat your hand against your hip. If your pup is ignoring you, be more animated with your voice. If that doesn't work, hold a treat in your left hand to coax your pup to walk with you.

Easy Training Techniques

You can start basic training with your pup a few days after he comes home. Focus on teaching concepts; there will be plenty of time for formal training later.

Training Guidelines

- At first, keep your training sessions to five minutes; then gradually increase the time. Try to train a few times a day.

- Train in a quiet place with few distractions.

- When training, use an object that gets your puppy's attention, like a small treat or toy. I will always refer to this object as a "treat." For puppies, I recommend rewarding with a treat and praise.

- Say your command once in a normal yet firm voice; do not repeat the command.

- Always keep the training sessions positive, and follow them by doing something that the pup enjoys.

- Never hit your dog with your hands or any other object (such as a newspaper).

- To find a reputable trainer in your area call the Association of Pet Dog Trainers at 1-800-738-3647.

Basic Commands

"*Sit*" Stand in front of your dog. Hold a treat in your hand, and raise it just above and over your dog's head. He will naturally sit to get his head in a better position to reach the treat. As your dog starts to sit, say "Sit," and give the dog the treat as soon as he sits. Give lots of praise. If your puppy will not sit with this method, put one hand on the pup's rear and one hand under the chin. As you say "Sit," gently push down on the rear and lift up the chin. After the pup sits, reward with praise and a treat.

"*Down*" Stand in front of your dog. Hold a treat in your hand with your fingers closed. Put this hand in front of your dog's nose and get his attention. Bring your hand down to the ground with your palm facing down. The dog will naturally lie down to try to get the treat. As you bring your hand down, say the word "Down." Hold your hand there until the dog lies down. As soon as the dog is lying on the ground, give the dog the treat. Remember to give lots of praise.

If your dog doesn't go down, put the hand with the treat in front of your dog's nose, swiftly bring this hand down to the ground and in toward your dog's front paws, and say the word "Down." While doing this, you may have to place the other hand on the pup's back and gently push down. Again, keep your hand there until the dog lies down. Give the dog the treat once he goes down. Give lots of praise!

"*Come*" This is the most important command that you will ever teach your dog. It can potentially save your dog's life. Introduce this command gradually to a young pup. Always teach this command in a contained area, not in a park or an unfenced yard. Stand about ten feet away from the pup. Say your dog's name and then say "Come." If your pup doesn't respond, try raising the pitch of your voice and taking a couple of quick steps backwards. If he still doesn't come, clap your hands and bend down while you call your dog. You need to make the dog want to come to you. Always have a treat for your dog when he comes. The dog should come within your reach right away. Eventually, your goal should be to have your dog immediately come to you and sit in front of you. Never call your dog to punish him.

LEARNING COMMANDS

Command Word	Behavior	Date First Learned
"Sit"	Sit down	
"Down"	Lie down	
"Come"	Come to me when called	
"Off"	Get off of or get down from	
"Kennel"	Go into the crate	
"Let's go"	Move with me	
"Leave it"	Don't touch or chase it	
"Heel"	Walk at my left side	
"Gentle"	Be gentle	
"No bite"	Do not bite	
"Stay"	Do not move, until released	
"Release"	It's okay to move, after a "Stay"	
"Drop" or "Give"	Let go of it	
"Wait"	Hold still for a moment	
"OK"	Permission granted	

Pooch Pointer: Training a Dog

Always use your normal voice with a firm tone when training your dog. You do not want to have to yell to get your dog to respond to your commands. During your training sessions, mix up the sequence of your commands so that you keep your dog's attention.

Pooch Pointer: Beginning Obedience Class and Canine Good Citizen Test

Once your dog is four to five months of age, you should consider taking a beginning obedience class. After completing the class, consider taking your dog for the Canine Good Citizen Test. With a little work, any dog can obtain this certificate from the American Kennel Club (AKC). According to the AKC, the purpose of this test is to ensure that our dogs can be respected members of the community. This test isn't a competition; it is merely a test of your dog's manners. The training is not only fun, but it also creates a closer bond between you and your dog. Call the AKC at 1-919-852-3875 for more information, or visit their web site: www.akc.org.

PERSONALITY TRAITS

When I give my dog a bath . . . .

. . . .

. . . .

. . . .

. . . .

. . . .

. . . .

My dog refuses . . . .

. . . .

. . . .

. . . .

. . . .

. . . .

. . . .

A very strange thing my dog does is . . . .

. . . .

. . . .

. . . .

. . . .

. . . .

. . . .

. . . .

My dog is afraid of . . . .
. . . .
. . . .
. . . .
. . . .
. . . .

My dog drives me crazy when . . . .
. . . .
. . . .
. . . .
. . . .
. . . .

EVERYDAY DELIGHTS

TRICKS AND GAMES

My dog's best tricks are . . . .

. . . .

. . . .

. . . .

My dog loves to play . . . .

. . . .

. . . .

. . . .

A great game we made up is . . . .

. . . .

. . . .

. . . .

Pooch Pointer: Hide-and-Seek

Get one of your dog's favorite toys. Ask your dog to sit, and then let him smell the toy. Tell your dog "Stay," and go hide the toy out of his sight (for the first few times, don't make the game too challenging). Return to your dog and say "Find it." Once he finds the toy and brings it to you, reward him with a treat. If your dog is having trouble with the game, try hiding a treat; this should give the dog more incentive to play the game.

BEHAVIORS AND MANNERISMS

To get my attention, my dog . . . .

. . . .

. . . .

. . . .

When I walk in the door, my dog greets me by . . . .

. . . .

. . . .

. . . .

When someone rings the doorbell, my dog . . . .

. . . .

. . . .

. . . .

When my dog sees another dog . . . .

. . . .

. . . .

. . . .

When my dog sees a cat . . . .

. . . .

. . . .

. . . .

Dog's Favorites

Toys . . . .
. . . .
. . . .
. . . .

Friends . . . .
. . . .
. . . .
. . . .

Foods . . . .
. . . .
. . . .
. . . .

Places to nap . . . .
. . . .
. . . .
. . . .

Pooch Pointer: Toy Making

Take an empty plastic bottle and place a handful of kibble in it. Put some nontoxic glue on the inside grooves of the cap. Tighten the cap and let the glue dry. This toy should only be given under supervision to prevent the dog from shredding the plastic and swallowing it.

Doggie Treats

Doggie Birthday Cake

1 lb. ground meat

2 slices whole wheat bread, torn into pieces

½ cup skim milk

1 cup rolled oats or Total® cereal

1 egg

200 IU vitamin E

¼ cup corn nibblets, drained

½ tsp. garlic

¼ cup cheddar cheese

¼ cup honey

Preheat oven to 350°. Mix the ingredients together. Bake at 350° for 25–30 minutes in an 8-inch pie plate, until no pink is left. You can decorate the top of the cake with kibble or your dog's favorite treats. Cool completely before serving. Serves about 8 dogs. Make sure to cut into pieces and serve each dog away from the others. Store leftovers in the refrigerator.

Canine Cookies

2¼ cups whole wheat flour

1 egg (beaten)

¼ cup wheat germ

1 tbsp. molasses

½ cup skim milk

½ cup rolled oats

¼ tsp. garlic powder

½ lb. liver

¼ tsp. salt

200 IU vitamin E

Preheat oven to 375°. Combine all dry ingredients. Process liver in food processor until it makes a thick paste. Warning: Mixing the liver can look a bit gross. Mix liver, milk, molasses, and egg into dry ingredients. Knead mixture into a ball until it is the consistency of pie dough. Roll into a ¼-inch-thick rectangle between two pieces of floured waxed paper. Cut dough into ½-inch by 1-inch strips. Place on greased cookie sheet. Bake at 375° for 10 minutes; turn cookies over and bake another 15 minutes. Cool cookies thoroughly before giving to your dog. Keep cookies in refrigerator or freeze some. Cookies will last in refrigerator for about 2 weeks.

DOGGIE FRIENDS

PUPPY'S FIRST BIRTHDAY

TODAY . . . . , WE CELEBRATED

THE FIRST BIRTHDAY OF . . . . , OUR BELOVED DOG.

This joyous occasion was commemorated . . . .

. . . .

. . . .

This event was shared with . . . .

. . . .

. . . .

. . . .

. . . .

Pooch Pointer: Birthday Party Game

Have your dog sit in front of three plastic cups. Show your dog that you are placing a treat under one of the cups. Move the cups around. Tell your dog to "Find it." If your dog knocks over or otherwise chooses the cup with the treat in it, he gets to eat it. If he doesn't guess the right cup, start the game again or give him the treat anyway because it's his birthday.

FIRST BIRTHDAY MEMORIES

BIRTHDAY MEMORIES

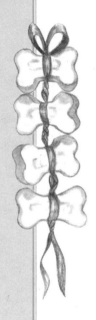

HOLIDAY WARNINGS

WE OFTEN OVERLOOK THE POTENTIAL DANGERS of festive celebrations for our dogs. Treat the safety of your dog just like you would treat that of a toddler during these events.

Guests

- Make sure guests know not to let the dog out if they aren't supposed to.

- Inform your guests not to feed the dog. They may inadvertently feed the dog something that can be toxic to him (e.g., chocolate).

Gifts

- Gifts decorated with special trimmings can be a choking hazard to your dog.

- Pick up gift wrapping soon after opening gifts.

Decorations

- If you celebrate Christmas and your dog doesn't do well around the tree, restrict the dog's access to the tree. Beware—tinsel or icicles can be a deadly hazard if swallowed.

- Make sure that lights, cords, stockings, and garlands are tacked down.

- Place all candles and menorahs out of the way of a curious nose or wagging tail.

- On the Fourth of July, make sure that your dog isn't within reach of sparklers or fireworks.

Festive Plants

■ Be careful where you choose to display holiday plants. Poinsettias, mistletoe, and holly are toxic to your dog.

Food

■ Make sure all the garbage is secure. Never leave food or candy, even wrapped, under the Christmas tree, within reach of the dog.

■ When cooking, pay careful attention to curious dogs.

■ On Halloween or Easter, make sure your dog doesn't find your children's goodies.

FIRST HOLIDAYS

HOLIDAY MEMORIES

....
....
....
....
....
....
....
....
....
....
....
....
....
....
....
....
....
....
....
....
....
....

HOLIDAY MOMENTS

CANINE FANCIES AND FANTASIES

If you could discover your dog's thoughts and wildest dreams, what do you think they would be? . . . .

Has your dog ever wagged his tail or barked while he was asleep? What do you think he was dreaming about? . . . .

When I leave the house, my dog . . . .

My dog's perfect day would be spent . . . .
. . . .
. . . .
. . . .
. . . .
. . . .

My dog chases his tail because . . . .
. . . .
. . . .
. . . .
. . . .
. . . .

If a Dog Were Your Teacher

You would learn stuff like . . .

When a loved one returns home, run to greet them.

Let others know when they have invaded your space.

Run, romp, and play daily.

Avoid biting, when a simple growl will do.

On hot days, drink lots of water and lay under a shady tree.

No matter how often you're scolded, don't buy into the guilt thing and pout.

Delight in the simple joy of a long walk.

Eat with gusto and enthusiasm. Stop when you have had enough.

Be loyal.

Never pretend to be something you are not.

If what you want lies buried, dig until you find it.

—AUTHOR UNKNOWN

ODE TO CANINE THOUGHT

If I like it, it's mine.
If it's in my mouth, it's mine.
If I can take it from you, it's mine.
If I had it a little while ago, it's mine.
If I'm chewing something up, all the pieces are mine.
If it just looks like it's mine, it's mine.
If I saw it first, it's mine.
If you are playing with something and you put it down,
it automatically becomes mine.
If it's broken, it's yours.

—AUTHOR UNKNOWN

The Celebration of the Dog

All of the good things that have come to me
have come through my dog.

—A dog owner overheard in New York's Central Park

I am grateful for my dog . . . .
. . . .
. . . .
. . . .
. . . .
. . . .
. . . .

My dog reminds me to appreciate . . . .
. . . .
. . . .
. . . .
. . . .
. . . .
. . . .
. . . .

The most important lesson I have learned . . . .
. . . .
. . . .
. . . .
. . . .
. . . .
. . . .
. . . .

All knowledge, the totality of
all questions and all answers,
is contained in the dog.
—FRANZ KAFKA

MY DOG AND ME

FAVORITE MEMORIES

. . . .

. . . .

. . . .

. . . .

. . . .

. . . .

. . . .

. . . .

. . . .

. . . .

. . . .

. . . .

. . . .

REMEMBER WHEN

To Crate Train or Not to Crate Train

CRATE TRAINING IS EXTREMELY USEFUL for various reasons:

- It is a great training device for housebreaking your pup—a puppy will not eliminate where she sleeps. Thus, the puppy will eventually learn to "hold it" until you let her out of the crate.

- It allows you to travel with your pup safely, in either a car or an airplane.

- It provides a safe environment when you can't watch your pup, either at home or at an outdoor function (e.g., picnic or athletic event).

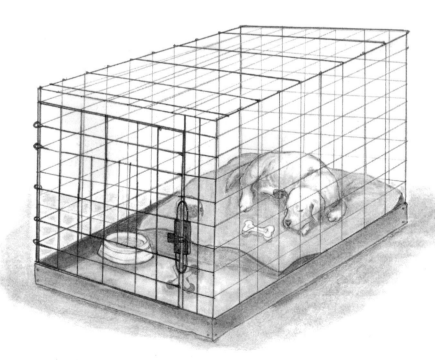

When buying a crate, consider how big your dog will be at maturity. Your dog should be able to stretch out and turn around in the crate even when fully grown.

You really have two options if you have a medium or large breed. The first is to buy a crate big enough for your dog's full size. While she is a puppy, you may have to section off part of the crate, so that the puppy does not sleep on one half of the crate and eliminate on the other half. This can be tricky, so take extra care to ensure that it is done safely.

A better option is to have two crates, a smaller one for when the dog is a puppy and a larger one for her full-grown size. To cut down on the expense, borrow the smaller size from a friend or check your local paper for a used crate for sale.

> ## Pooch Pointer:
> ## Toys and Water in the Crate
>
> *During the day, keep a small bowl with a few ice cubes in the crate. The ice will melt slowly; thus there is less of a chance that the pup will knock over the bowl and get the crate wet. Also, remember to give the pup a safe chew toy to play with while in the crate.*

I have two crates in my house: one is in my bedroom and one is in my living room. This way my dog has a place to sleep upstairs and downstairs.

(Note: You can take the doors of the crate off when your dog doesn't need to be kept in the crate; this way she can come and go as she pleases.)

How to Crate Train

- Clean the crate out with antibacterial soap. Place the crate in the area where you will be keeping it. Start off with an old towel in the bottom of the crate.

- Keep the door open, and let the dog explore the crate. Do not force the pup into the crate. Place some food or a toy in the back of the crate to entice the pup to go in. As the dog goes in, use a command, such as "Kennel," so that the dog will learn to associate going in the crate with the command. Repeat this several times.

- With the door open, feed the dog in the crate a few times. This will create a pleasant connection in the dog's mind with being in the crate. Then feed the dog in the crate with the door closed. Only do this for two or three meals. After feeding, take the pup outside to go potty.

- Once the dog is comfortable in the crate with the door closed for a minute, gradually start to increase the time. Have a toy in the crate to occupy the pup. Continue to reward the puppy for being in the crate—this reinforces positive behavior.

- Never let a whining or barking dog out of the crate, unless you think he has to go potty. Let the dog calm down for a full five minutes before taking him out. This avoids the connection in the dog's mind that if he whines or barks, he will be let out.

- If all is going well, keep increasing the amount of time your pup spends in the crate.

- While crate training is important, the crate is not a "puppy prison"; it is a tool to be used appropriately. Your pup needs to bond and adapt to living with you, not to living in the crate.

- The crate becomes the pup's safe place and needs to be respected as such. In addition, the crate is never to be used as punishment.

Pooch Pointer: Dog's Collar

Never leave your pup's collar on while he is in the crate because the collar might get caught on the crate and choke him.

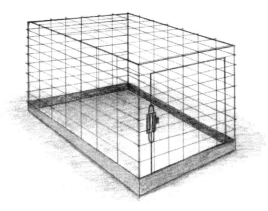

Taking Your Dog on a Road Trip (or Not)

Trip Guidelines

- Travel with your pet in a crate.

- Gradually acclimate the dog to riding in the car.

- Pay careful attention to the weather outside. Even in mild weather, the temperature in your car can rise to dangerous levels within minutes, even with your windows open. In cold conditions, provide your dog with a blanket for warmth.

- Avoid leaving your dog unattended in the car.

- Whenever you stop for a potty break, let your dog out to go potty.

- If your dog gets carsick, do not feed him for six hours prior to the trip. However, do not restrict water intake.

What to Bring

- The dog's first aid kit, see page 100

  - Crate with a pad in it

  - Dog's food and dish

  - Dog treats

  - Plenty of water for the ride

- Leashes and collars

- Dog towels and a few old sheets to protect bedding or furniture at your destination

- Favorite toys

- Plastic bags to pick up after the dog

- A list of your emergency numbers, including the vet

- A temporary ID tag for where you are going to be staying

- Your dog's current health records and rabies certificate, if you're crossing state lines

If your dog doesn't travel well or if your travel destination is not dog-friendly, it may be best to leave the dog home with a family member or with a dog sitter. You can request a referral from Pet Sitters International at 1-800-268-SITS. Another option is to board your dog. Call the American Boarding Kennels Association in Colorado Springs at 1-719-591-1113 for a referral.

> ## Pooch Pointer: A Cure for Car Sickness
>
> *Buy some ginger capsules, they usually come in 500 mg. For dogs over 15 pounds, sprinkle the whole capsule over 1 tablespoon of canned dog food or your dog's favorite people food (yogurt, peanut butter, etc.). For dogs under 15 pounds, use half the capsule.*

VACATION ESCAPADES

ADVENTURES

AGGRESSIVE BEHAVIORS

AGGRESSIVE BEHAVIORS MUST BE NIPPED in the bud. It is critical to let your puppy know that aggression will not be tolerated. Correcting aggressive behavior in a puppy (8–1 2 weeks old) will be easier than correcting aggressive behavior in an older dog. If you have adopted an older dog, do not attempt to correct extremely aggressive behavior yourself, as you might make the problem worse or get seriously injured—seek the advice of a professional behaviorist.

AGGRESSIVE BEHAVIORS TO BE AVOIDED

- Never let your puppy mouth, bite, or nip at any adult or child.

- Strongly discourage your puppy from continuing to display dominant behavior over a child or another puppy (e.g., mounting, standing over, playing too rough).

- Strongly discourage your pup from being possessive with food or toys around people or other dogs. Periodically take the pup's toy away; ask your dog to sit, and then after a few seconds give the toy back to the pup. Praise the pup for his good behavior. You can do the same thing with the dog's food dish.

Pooch Pointer: Approaching an Unfamiliar Dog

Approach an unfamiliar dog with caution. If you are interested in letting the dogs play, or even just letting them greet each other, ask the owner of the other dog if the dog is friendly or aggressive toward other dogs. Do not assume that the other dog is friendly.

Emergency Warning Signs

You are the first line of defense in your dog's good health. It is vital that you learn to recognize normal dog behavior so you can get veterinary help promptly if something goes wrong.

Signs of Illness

- Weight loss

- Behavior change

- Lethargy

- Increased water consumption (a lot more than normal)

- Obvious cough, vomiting, or diarrhea

Emergency Signs

- Trouble breathing and increased heart rate

- Vomiting and diarrhea for more than a day, especially multiple vomiting over a four- to six-hour period

- Loss of appetite for more than a day

- Suspicion that the dog has eaten anything toxic or has swallowed a sharp object

- Noticeably bloated abdomen

- Loss of consciousness

- Heat stroke

- Excessive bleeding/deep wounds

- Burns or broken bone

- Electrical shock

- Seizures

- Blood in urine, feces, or vomit

Pooch Pointer:
Pet Rescue Sticker

Display a pet rescue sign or sticker by the entrances to your home. This will alert emergency personnel that you have animals in the home. You can find rescue stickers at most local pet supply stores.

Dog First Aid Kit

CREATING A FIRST AID KIT FOR YOUR PET is imperative, and it's simple to do. Make one for home and one for the car. Familiarize family members and anyone watching the dog with the kit and its location.

You can find first aid kits at pet supply stores, you can order them through catalogs, or you can even create a kit yourself. It's important that the contents be clearly labeled, organized, and available at a moment's notice in one container. Any box will work, but a plastic storage container with a handle—like a sewing kit or tackle box—is ideal. Label it "Dog First Aid" in permanent marker. Tape important contact information, in permanent ink, to the inside lid:

- Your name, address, phone number, and e-mail address

- The name, address, and phone number of an emergency contact person

- The name, address, and phone number of your veterinarian

- The phone number of the Pet Poison Control hotline

For each dog that you have, make a card that includes his individual information:

- Dog's name, breed, description, microchip ID number (if any)

- Known health problems

- Dosages for specific medicines in the kit

Before administering any of the following over-the-counter drugs, contact your veterinarian for the correct dosages for your dog. Watch your dog for any allergic reactions he may have to any of the following medications.

Note: Never give your dog Tylenol® or ibuprofen (Advil®, Nuprin®, Motrin®, etc.). These can be toxic to dogs.

Fill in the dosage column with your veterinarian, and ask for any recommended additions to the kit. (Use additional space for other medications.)

Medicine/Equipment	Treatment for / Used for	Dosage (*consult vet for correct dosage)
Teaspoon and tablespoon	Measuring medicine	
Round-tip scissors	Cutting hair and bandages	
Liquid and pill syringe	Administering oral medicine	
Rectal thermometer	Checking temperature	
Bulb syringe	Flushing wounds	
Triple antibiotic ointment	Dressing wounds	
Instant cold pack	Reducing swelling	
Tweezers	Removing foreign objects	
Sterilized pads and tape	Covering wounds	
Gold Bond® powder	Skin irritation ("hot spots")	Cover affected area
Kwik Stop® (optional)	Stopping bleeding of minor cuts	See package for directions
Syrup of ipecac*	Inducing vomiting	
Ascriptin®*	Relieving pain	
Kaopectate®*	Controlling diarrhea	
Benadryl®*	Allergic reactions (bee stings)	

HOMEMADE REMEDIES

THE FOLLOWING REMEDIES HAVE WORKED well in my experience. However, please be aware that your dog may not react well to these treatments. Thus, please consult your veterinarian before using any of these remedies because your vet best knows the state of your dog's health.

The Frozen Pea Trick

A bag of frozen peas is a perfect ice pack because it molds to the dog's body—great to heal bruises and kill the pain of a strain or sprain.

Flea, Tick, Mosquito, and Fly Repellent

INGREDIENTS (use full strength): tea tree oil, rosemary oil, sage oil, cedarwood oil, peppermint oil, sweet orange oil, eucalyptus oil, citronella oil, pine needle oil.

SHAMPOO DIRECTIONS: Mix 4 drops of each oil with 32 ounces of any natural shampoo. Use as needed.

SPRAY DIRECTIONS: Mix 4 drops of each oil with 16 ounces of water in a spray bottle. Shake before each application, and spray lightly over entire body. Can use once a day, if needed.

Ear Wash for After Swimming

INGREDIENTS: white vinegar and rubbing alcohol

DIRECTIONS: Mix 8 ounces of white vinegar and 8 ounces of rubbing alcohol in an open-mouth bottle. Store with cap on the bottle.

APPLICATION: For each of your dog's ears, hold the bottle to the ear and quickly tip the bottle into the ear.

Spray to Protect Against Parvovirus

INGREDIENTS: bleach and water

DIRECTIONS: Mix 16 ounces of water with 2 tablespoons of bleach in a spray bottle.

APPLICATION: Before anyone enters any area where the puppy is allowed, spray solution on the bottoms of people's shoes and visiting dogs' paws.

Deskunking*

INGREDIENTS: 1 quart 3% hydrogen peroxide, ¼ cup baking soda (sodium bicarbonate), and 1 tsp. liquid soap

DIRECTIONS: Begin by wetting the animal down; then apply the mixture, and work it through the animal's hair. Leave the solution on 3 to 4 minutes, and finish with a tap water rinse.

*CAUTION: Only prepare one treatment of this at a time, and throw away any excess, as it is unsafe to store this combination of chemicals. *Recipe invented by Paul Krebaum.*

Pooch Pointer: Bringing Home a Second Pet—The Sweet Smell of a Friend

Cats and dogs identify friend and foe by scent. Ease the transition by making the new and resident pets smell alike—dab on a bit of vanilla extract under each animal's chin and at the base of their tails.

Medical History

Veterinarian

Name . . . .

Address . . . .

. . . .

Phone . . . .

Allergies

. . . .

. . . .

Spayed/Neutered

Date . . . .

Performed by . . . .

Pooch Pointer: Spaying and Neutering

If you are not planning to show or breed your dog, you should strongly consider having your dog spayed/ neutered before six months of age.

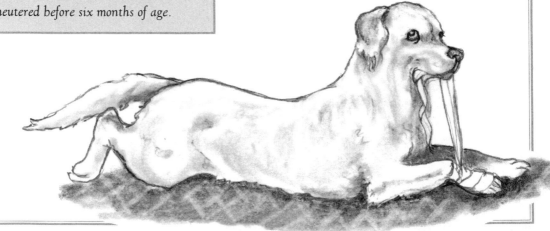

MEDICAL RECORD CHART

Date	Problem	Treatment Prescribed	Vet

VACCINATION RECORD

ON YOUR INITIAL VISIT TO YOUR VETERINARIAN, ask about the recommended schedule of vaccinations. Keeping your puppy's vaccinations up-to-date helps keep your dog as healthy as possible. Also, inquire about your town's or county's licensing requirements.

Until your pup is vaccinated against parvovirus, it is very important to protect your pup against this disease. Ask your veterinarian how to protect your pup from it. For a homemade preventative suggestion, see page 103.

NAME OF VACCINE	PROTECTION AGAINST	DATE(S) ADMINISTERED	EXPIRATION DATE

IMPORTANT PHONE NUMBERS AND INFORMATION

ONCE YOU HAVE FILLED IN THIS PAGE, make a photocopy of it, or type this into a computer document and print out the information. Tape this sheet of paper to your refrigerator. Make sure everyone knows where this information is located.

OWNER'S CONTACT INFORMATION	OTHER CONTACT INFORMATION
Name	Veterinarian . . . .
Address	
. . . .	Emergency contact . . . .
. . . .	
Phone	Breeder . . . .
E-mail	

ASPCA NATIONAL ANIMAL POISON CONTROL CENTER:

1-800-548-2423 (charge on credit card)

1-900-680-0000 (charge to your phone bill)

DOG'S IMPORTANT INFORMATION

Call name . . . .

Breed . . . . Markings . . . .

AKC registration name (if any) . . . .

AKC registration number (if any) . . . .

Microchip ID number (if any) . . . .

RECOMMENDED BOOKS AND WEB SITES

BEHAVIOR AND TRAINING BOOKS

How to Raise a Puppy You Can Live With (Alpine Publications) by Clarice Rutherford
and David H. Neil

Don't Shoot the Dog (Bantam Books) by Karen Pryor

How To Teach A New Dog Old Tricks (James & Kenneth) by Dr. Ian Dunbar

HEALTH AND CARE BOOKS

New Choices in Natural Healing for Dogs & Cats (Rodale) by Amy D. Shojai

U. C. Davis Book of Dogs (HarperCollins) by U. C. Davis School of Veterinary Medicine Staff,
Edited by Mordecai Siegal

The Humane Society of the United States Complete Guide to Dog Care (Little, Brown and Co.)
by Marion S. Lane and HSUS Staff

ASPCA Complete Guide to Dogs (Chronicle Books) by Sheldon L. Gerstenfeld with
Jacque Linn Schultz

GENERAL-INTEREST BOOKS

Dogs for Dummies (IDG Books Worldwide) by Gina Spadafori

Pack of Two (The Dial Press) by Caroline Knapp

Cooking with Dogs (Two Dog Press) by Karen Dowell

CANINE WEB SITES

There are so many good Web sites out there, but here are a few you might want to check out:

www.avma.org	American Veterinary Medical Association
www.thepoop.com	Training, health, and behavior issues
www.pets.com	PetVets—Training, health, and behavior issues
www.cyberpet.com	A range of topics (nutrition, rescue organizations, pet chat room)
www.dog-play.com	Suggestions of fun activities to do with your dog
www.canismajor.com	Online dog magazine that covers everything from housetraining to food and nutrition

PET SUPPLY CATALOGS

Name	Telephone Number	Web Site
Arcata Pet	1-800-822-9085	www.arcatapet-online.com
Care A Lot	1-800-343-7680	www.carealot.org
Doctors Foster & Smith	1-800-826-7206	www.drsfostersmith.com
Jeffers	1-800-533-3377	www.jefferspet.com
New England Serum Co.	1-800-637-3786	www.NESerum.com
Noah's Pet Supplies	1-888-NOAHS PET	www.noahspets.com
Omaha Vaccine	1-800-367-4444	www.omahavaccine.com
Pedigrees	1-800-548-4786	n/a
Petopia	1-877-PETOPIA	www.petopia.com
Pets.com	1-888-321-7387	www.pets.com
Pet Warehouse	1-800-443-1160	www.petwhse.com
R. C. Steele	1-800-872-3773	www.rcsteele.com

Pooch Pointer:
Making a "Lost Dog" Sign

If your dog gets lost, first call local shelters to see if your dog was taken there. If necessary, make a "Lost Dog" sign and display it in as many places as you can, even in mailboxes. Make sure to: place a recent color picture of your dog on the sign; print the flyer on bright yellow paper with black ink; put the sign in a sheet protector if hanging outdoors. Include the following information: dog's name, age, and gender; any markings; owner's phone numbers and e-mail address (do not put any additional contact information); date lost; the location the dog was last seen. If you're offering a reward, say so, but do not say how much.

In Loving Memory

It is in celebration of the life of

. . . .

that I record and honor the cherished memories
and knowledge gained by knowing such a great being.
Our wonderful journey began on

. . . .

And today

. . . .

marks the day that my friend
leaves this world for another.

A MEMORIAL TRIBUTE

Some of the wisdom that I gained from knowing . . . .

. . . .

. . . .

. . . .

. . . .

. . . .

My most cherished memories . . . .

. . . .

. . . .

. . . .

. . . .

. . . .

. . . .

. . . .

. . . .

. . . .

The bond with a true dog is as lasting
as the ties of this earth can ever be.
—KONRAD LORENZ

About the Author

Lorie Glantz has shared her life with animals for over 20 years. Currently, she resides in Burlington, Massachusetts, with her husband, son, and Golden Retriever. She is also the author of *My Cat's Tale*. For more information about enriching your life with your dog, or to contact Lorie, go to www.mydogstale.com.

About the Illustrator

Emily Youngreen is an artist with over 30 years of experience in illustration, oil painting, watercolor, and more. She has recently completed *When Mommy Sings to the Forest,* a moving and mystical children's book. She currently lives in British Columbia, Canada.